All By Myself

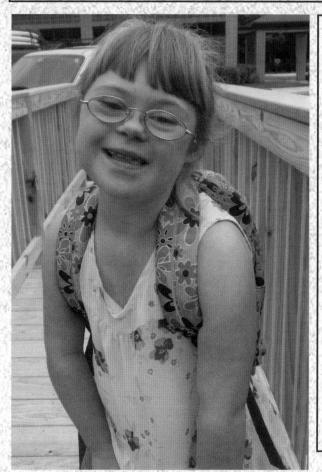

Snapshots of a Child with Down Syndrome Learning the Value of Independence

Written & Photographed by

Shelly Miller

To Rachael Kay Miller.
Your life has blessed us in more ways
than we could ever imagine!

To all the doctors, therapists, and teachers
who make it possible for children with disabilities to
live independent lives. Your dedication is greatly
admired, and your service is deeply appreciated.

ISBN-13: 978-1496192998
ISBN-10: 1496192990

Printed by CreateSpace, An Amazon.com Company

Dear Reader,

This book was written for our daughter, Rachael and given to her as a gift to celebrate her achievements. We wanted to communicate that, although her disability limits her in some ways, she is overcoming it with motivation, perseverance, therapy, and lots of practice. Furthermore, we value her persistence to do things *all by herself*, even if it requires a little help or if it is not done perfectly.

When we shared this book with parents, teachers, librarians, and therapists, the feedback was very positive. It was suggested that Rachael's story could benefit others in a number of ways. For example, it could inform new parents of children with Down syndrome that their child is capable of achieving success in many areas of life, advise family and friends that the challenges these children face can be overcome, and communicate to peers that they have a lot in common with children who have Down syndrome. As a result, this book was published so others can use it as a resource for children with Down syndrome, their parents, family members, and friends. We hope it provides a sense of understanding and hope, knowing that your loved one can achieve great things on their journey towards independence!

Many blessings,

Keven & Shelly Miller

YAWN, I stretch my arms and rub my eyes. Time to wake up. I pull on my window shade. *FFFLIP!* It goes up like a shot!

I look out the window. The sun is not up yet, but I am! I turn on my light and find my friends.

"What are we doing today?" bunny says. "We go to school!" says lamb. "Let's have a great day!" I say, as I give my friends a big hug.

When I am done playing, I climb back into bed. *THUNK!* The door flies open. In comes my little sister. "Hello Rebecca", I say. "Do you want me to read you a story?" "Sure!" she replies.

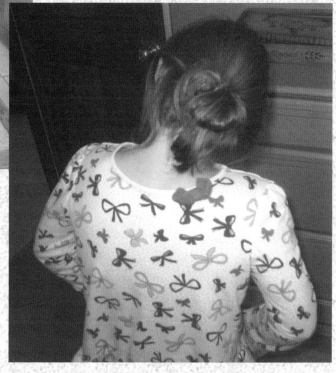

"Time to get ready for your day!" calls Mom from the hallway. It's time to brush my teeth and put on my clothes. Sometimes I need help, but I try to do it all by myself.

Sometimes I put my shirt or my pants on backwards. Mom chuckles and helps me get it right.

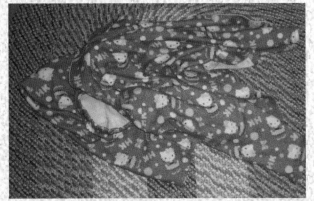

Other times I leave my pajamas on the floor. Mom frowns and tells me to pick them up.

It's time to brush my hair. I don't like to do it, but Mom says it's important that I look my best. "What hairstyle do you want?" Mom asks. I tell her what I say *every* day, "ponytail, please." My mom is a good sport, she does just what I ask.

Hello! My name is Rachael, and I have Down syndrome. That means I was born with one extra chromosome in each one of my tiny cells. Most people have 46 chromosomes. I have 47.

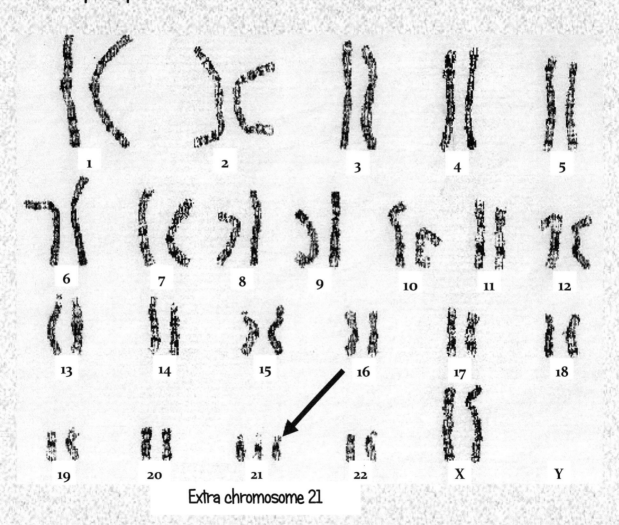

Extra chromosome 21

Because of this, some things are more difficult for me to do. I have to try harder and practice more. Sometimes I need a little help.

I have special teachers called therapists who teach me how to do things. My speech therapist teaches me how to say words clearly.

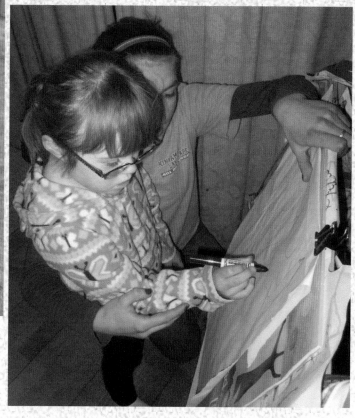

My PT teaches me how to use my big muscles so I can do things like kick a ball. My OT teaches me how to use my small muscles so I can do things like write my name.

Sometimes I don't want to go to therapy, but my parents tell me it's important because I am learning how to be *INDEPENDENT.*

It also helps me to do the *FUN* things like gymnastics, swimming, and playing with my friends on the playground.

After I get ready in the morning, I race my sister to the kitchen. My sister beats me, but that's OK. "I will let you win next time!" she says. I really *adore* my sister.

"What do you want for breakfast?" Mom asks. I say, "I want oatmeal. I can help!" I pour the milk. SPLAT! It spills all over. "Oh my word, I made a mess!" That's ok. I will wipe it up.

"Yum-a", I say as I carry the warm bowl of oatmeal to the table. When I'm done eating, I put my dishes on the counter. Mom says it's very important that I clean up after myself.

Time to go to school! I get my things ready for the bus. I try to do it all by myself.

When I put on my coat, my arm just won't go in. "Arrr! I cry. I can't do it!" Mom tells me to take a deep breath. "A-haa!" I say. I feel better now. Mom gives me my coat so I can try again. I get it this time! Now I can go outside, and catch the bus!

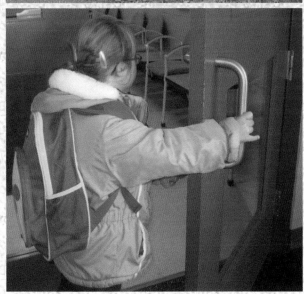

REWARD!

When I get to school, I do my best to listen and follow directions. It feels great when I get my work done, and I earn a reward!

When I come home from school, I help Mom set the table for dinner. Then, I read a book.

When Dad comes home, I say "Look Dad I set the table!" Dad smiles and tells me that I did a great job. He says that it is important that I help Mom.

After supper, Dad helps me with my homework. I do my best to get it all done.

Then it's time to get ready for bed. I brush my teeth, put on my pajamas, and climb into bed. I try to do it all by myself.

Dad reads to me, and then we say a prayer. My eyes get heavy. Dad tells me that I am loved just as I am.

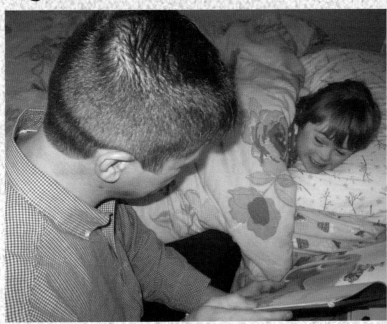

"Thank you, Daddy," I whisper as I drift off to sleep...

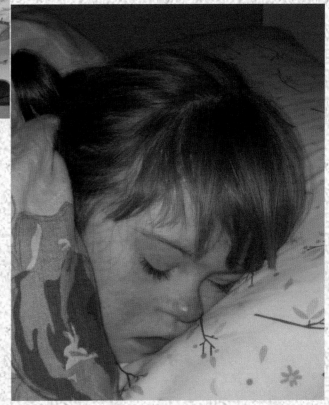

About the Author

Shelly Miller is a graduate of Providence College where she received a Bachelor of Science degree in Management. She earned her Master of Arts degree in Elementary Education at Towson University in Maryland, and she worked in the teaching profession before leaving the workforce to raise a family.

Shelly is a devoted wife and mother of two beautiful children, Rachael and Rebecca. She is passionate about getting the word out to prospective parents on the benefits of having children with Down syndrome. Shelly enjoys sharing with others that "Rachael is a happy, lovable, adorable little girl who makes me smile often every day. She brings out the best in me. As a result, my faith in God has grown, and I am a more patient, loving, caring person. I encourage everyone to embrace the opportunity to experience blessings like that!

Quotes from Readers:

"*All By Myself* helps answer some of the questions children with Down syndrome have about their disability and how they can deal with the challenges they are faced with. It offers encouragement to the reader as they experience Rachael doing normal, everyday kinds of activities with persistence and happiness!"
–Linda, Parent of child with Down syndrome

"This book is a powerful resource for educating friends, family, classmates, teachers, and families about the importance of understanding individuals that learn at their own pace and the power of perseverance in reaching their potential. Inspiring, uplifting and moving, *All By Myself* belongs on the shelf of every classroom, library, doctor, and therapist's office." –Amy, Occupational Therapist R/L

"The greatest asset when attempting to aid any child is information, which is exactly what this book delivers. The reader is given practical, insightful information as they experience Rachael's efforts to complete her daily activities. *All by Myself* offers perspective, hope, and joy as the reader is exposed to Rachael's world." -Shayna, Speech and Language Pathologist

"As a Special Education Teacher, I often explain to the students visiting the classroom that they have a lot in common with my students. *All by Myself* uses real life experiences to get that point across in a heartfelt way. I would highly recommend it to all inclusive classroom teachers who want to help their students understand one another." – Sheri, Special Education Teacher

"This story is one that can be read to other children and related to in a positive way. With discussion, it can be easily concluded that Rachael has the same experiences, challenges, and responsibilities as her peers. *All By Myself* is a must have for every classroom library." -Sandy, Elementary Education Teacher

Lesson Plan: *All By Myself*

Objective: To help students understand that similarities outweigh the differences between children with Down syndrome and their peers. To help peers understand some of the challenges these children face on a daily basis.

Materials: Book *All By Myself*, whiteboard **For Extension Activities:** mittens, pegboard and pegs in a bag, lacing activity, emotions on index cards, children's blurry sunglasses (with gluestick on lenses)

Introduction: Read the title. What do you think this story will be about? Discuss the words snapshots and Down syndrome. Ask students to share what they know about Down syndrome.

Vocabulary:
Chuckled – to laugh quietly
Down syndrome – A condition caused by an extra chromosome on the 21st pair. It causes learning difficulties and certain physical characteristics.
Cells – very small units that all living things are made up of – people are made up of trillions of them
Chromosomes – each cell contains chromosomes that contain detailed instructions on how to make each of one of our body parts.
Independence – the ability to do things on our own
Therapist - a person trained to help people overcome challenges. PT-Physical Therapist, OT-Occupational Therapist

Read book and ask questions:
What are some of the routines you follow in the morning and at night?
What do you need help with? Does anyone help you out?
Are there some things that you don't feel like doing sometimes?
What are some of the favorite things that you do?
Do you do any chores around the house?

After reading ask questions:
What did you learn about Down syndrome?
Write on whiteboard: *SAME* and *DIFFERENT*
What are some things you all have in common with Rachael? List them under *SAME*
What is different between you and Rachael? List under *DIFFERENT*
Do you have more similarities or differences?

Closing: Children with Down syndrome may have more difficulty doing some activities, but they can be successful with perseverance, assistance, practice, and therapy. When compared with most children their age, they have more similarities than differences.

Extension activities:
Below are some ways that students can explore what it is like to have a disability. After completing each activity, ask them to describe what it was like. Discuss how it takes more time, patience, and focus to get the task done with limitations.
Peg Activity: The student will take pegs out of a bag and put them in a pegboard with and without mittens on.
Lacing Activity: The student will lace an object with and without blurry sunglasses on.
Writing Activity: The student will write their names with their dominant hand and opposite hand.
Emotion Activity: The student will choose an emotion index card and express it using their words and without using their words.

Made in the USA
Lexington, KY
30 August 2014